KT-524-607

TABLE OF Contents

Origami toy box.. 4

Materials 5

Folding techniques and symbols..................... 6

Basketball hoop... 8

Hungry crow 10

Royal crown 12

Air shark 14

Mini piano 16

Sumo wrestler 18

Bug-eyed darting frog 20

Origami playtime.. 22

Read more 24

Internet sites.. 24

ORIGAMI toy box

Peek inside the origami toy box!
You'll find a treasure chest loaded
with seven fun paper toys. Practise
your jump shot with a clever
basketball hoop. Send a pair of
paper sumo wrestlers into battle.
Challenge your friends to bug-eyed
darting frog races. Jump in, start
folding, and let the fun begin!

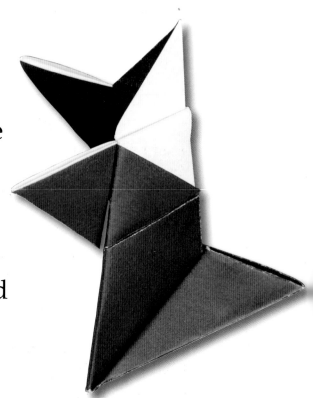

easy origami

EASY Origami TOYS

by christopher L. Harbo

Aberdeenshire

3077757

www.raintreepublishers.co.uk
Visit our website to find out
more information about
Raintree books.

To order:
☎ Phone 0845 6044371
🖷 Fax +44 (0) 1865 312263
🖳 Email myorders@raintreepublishers.co.uk

Customers from outside the UK please telephone +44 1865 312262

Raintree is an imprint of Capstone Global Library Limited, a company incorporated in England and Wales having its registered office at 7 Pilgrim Street, London, EC4V 6LB – Registered company number: 6695582

First published by Capstone Press in 2011
First published in the United Kingdom in 2012
The moral rights of the proprietor have been asserted.

All rights reserved. No part of this publication may be reproduced in any form or by any means (including photocopying or storing it in any medium by electronic means and whether or not transiently or incidentally to some other use of this publication) without the written permission of the copyright owner, except in accordance with the provisions of the Copyright, Designs and Patents Act 1988 or under the terms of a licence issued by the Copyright Licensing Agency, Saffron House, 6–10 Kirby Street, London EC1N 8TS (www.cla.co.uk). Applications for the copyright owner's written permission should be addressed to the publisher.

Photo Credits: Capstone Studio/Karon Dubke, all photos
Artistic Effects: Shutterstock/ Jackie Stukey, Nebojsa I, oorka, patrimonio designs limited, Petr Bukal, Skocko, SoleilC
Originated by Capstone Global Library Ltd
Printed and bound in China by Leo Paper Products Ltd

ISBN 978 1 406 24266 9
16 15 14 13 12
10 9 8 7 6 5 4 3 2 1

British Library Cataloguing in Publication Data
A full catalogue record for this book is available from the British Library.

Disclaimer
All the Internet addresses (URLs) given in this book were valid at the time of going to press. However, due to the dynamic nature of the Internet, some addresses may have changed, or sites may have changed or ceased to exist since publication. While the publisher regrets any inconvenience this may cause readers, no responsibility for any such changes can be accepted by the publisher.

ABOUT THE AUTHOR

Christopher L. Harbo loves origami. He began folding paper several years ago and hasn't stopped. In addition to decorative origami, he also enjoys folding paper aeroplanes. When he's not making origami, Christopher spends his free time reading Japanese comic books and watching films.

MATERIALS

Origami is a simple art that doesn't use many materials. You'll only need the following things to complete the projects in this book:

Origami paper: Square origami paper comes in many fun colours and sizes. You can use 15 by 15 centimetres square paper for the models in this book, unless the instructions tell you to use a different paper size. You can buy this paper in most craft shops.

A4-sized paper: Not all origami models begin with a square. Use A4 paper (210 by 297 millimetres) when needed.

Ruler: Some models use measurements to complete. A ruler will help you measure.

Pencil: Use a pencil when you need to mark spots you measure with the ruler.

Craft supplies: Pens and other craft supplies will help you to decorate your models.

FOLDING TECHNIQUES

Folding paper is easier when you understand basic origami folds and symbols. Practise the folds on this list before trying the models in this book. Turn back to this list if you get stuck on a tricky step, or ask an adult for help.

Valley Folds are represented by a dashed line. One side of the paper is folded against the other like a book. A sharp fold is made by running your finger along the fold line.

Mountain Folds are represented by a pink or white dashed and dotted line. The paper is folded sharply behind the model.

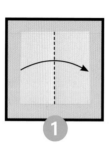

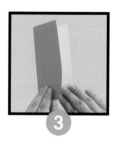

Squash Folds are formed by lifting one edge of a pocket. The pocket gets folded again so the spine gets flattened. The existing fold lines become new edges.

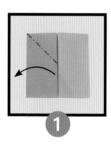

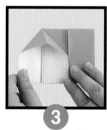

Inside reverse folds are made by opening a pocket slightly. Then you fold the model inside itself along existing fold lines.

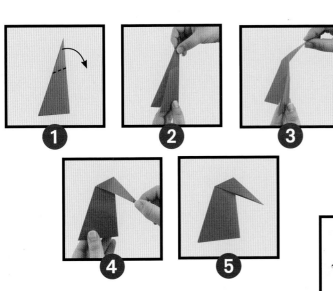

Outside reverse Folds are made by opening a pocket slightly. Then you fold the model outside itself along existing fold lines.

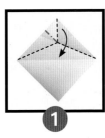

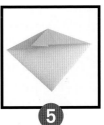

Rabbit ear Folds are formed by bringing two edges of a point together using existing fold lines. The new point is folded to one side.

SYMBOLS

SINGLE-POINTED ARROW:
Fold the paper in the direction of the arrow.

HALF-POINTED ARROW:
Fold the paper behind.

DOUBLE-POINTED ARROW:
Fold the paper and then unfold it.

LOOPING ARROW:
Turn the paper over or turn it to a new position.

BASKETBALL hoop

Traditional model

Get ready to shoot some hoops without ever leaving the table. Fold this basketball hoop and hold a free throwing contest.

1

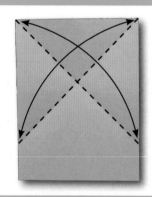

Start with an A4-sized piece of paper. Valley fold the top-left corner to the right edge and unfold. Valley fold the top-right corner to the left edge and unfold.

Turn the paper over.

2

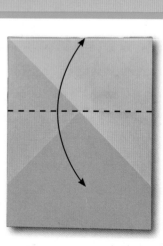

Valley fold the top edge down and unfold. Note that the corners should meet the ends of the folds from step 1.

3

4

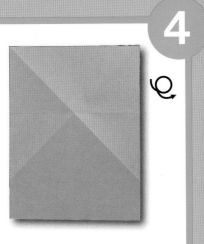

Turn the paper over.

5

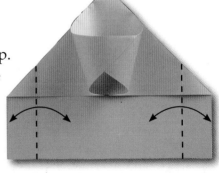

Use your finger to push down on the paper at point A. Grab the top edge of the paper and pull it towards the bottom on the fold lines. The top layer of the paper will form a triangle.

6

Curl the left and right points of the triangle towards each other. Tuck one point inside the other to form a hoop.

7

Valley fold the left and right edges even with the sides of the hoop. Then unfold the edges halfway.

8

Game on! Crumple a piece of paper into a ball and take your best shot at the hoop.

PLAY hint Place your hoop on the end of a long table. Practise shooting from the other end of the table. See how many baskets you can make in a row.

9

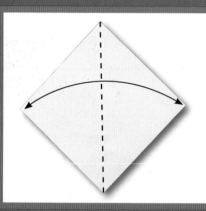

HUNGRY CROW

Traditional model

A hungry crow will search high and low for a meal. This model walks across the table as it pecks for food.

1

Start with the coloured side of the paper face down. Valley fold the left point to the right point and unfold.

2

Valley fold the top-left edge to the centre. Valley fold the top-right edge to the centre.

3

Valley fold the bottom point up. Make this fold along the edge made in step 2.

4

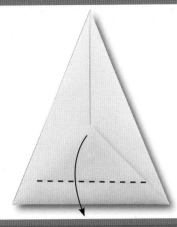

Valley fold the point past the bottom edge. Make this fold about 1·3 cm from the model's bottom edge.

5

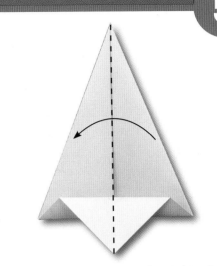

Valley fold the right side of the model to the left side.

6

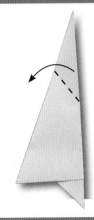

Valley fold the top point down and to the left. Run your finger firmly along the fold and then unfold the point.

7

Inside reverse fold the point on the folds from step 6. This fold allows the right edge of the point to swing inside the model. When finished, the point sticks out from the left side of the model.

Peck, peck, peck. Your hungry crow is ready to eat.

8

PLAY hint Tilt the crow so its beak rests on the table. Gently tap its tail to make the hungry crow walk and peck.

ROYAL Crown

Traditional model

Kings and queens need crowns to rule their kingdoms. Fold this simple model, and your royal head will never be bare.

1

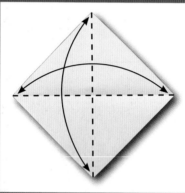

Start with the coloured side of the paper face down. Valley fold the left point to the right point and unfold. Valley fold the top point to the bottom point and unfold.

Turn the model over.

3

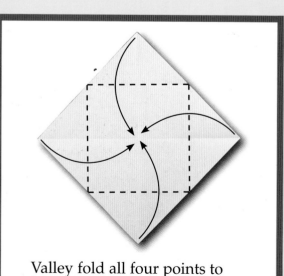

Valley fold all four points to the centre of the paper.

2

12

4

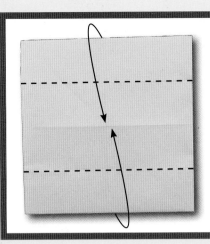

Valley fold the top and bottom edges to the centre fold. Allow the flaps behind the edges to swing to the front.

5

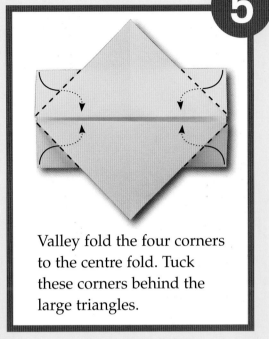

Valley fold the four corners to the centre fold. Tuck these corners behind the large triangles.

6

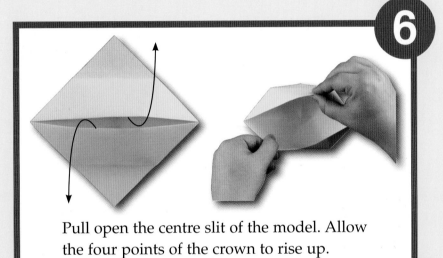

Pull open the centre slit of the model. Allow the four points of the crown to rise up.

7

Pinch the crown's corners to make the model square.

8

Wear your crown to be a king or queen for the day!

PLAY hint To wear this crown, make sure you start with a piece of paper large enough to fit your head. A 46 cm square of newspaper works best.

AIR shark

Traditional model

The air shark is no ordinary paper aeroplane. It hunts the skies with a large fin rising up from its back.

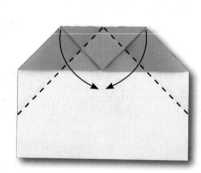

1

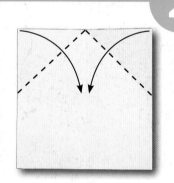

Start with the coloured side of the paper face down. Valley fold the left edge to the right edge and unfold.

2

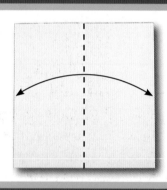

Valley fold the top-left corner to the centre fold. Valley fold the top-right corner to the centre fold.

Valley fold the top point to the edge made in step 2.

3

Valley fold the top-left edge to the centre. Valley fold the top-right edge to the centre.

4

5

Mountain fold the right side of the model behind the left side. Then turn the model so the tip points to the right.

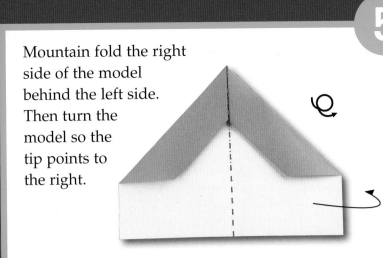

6

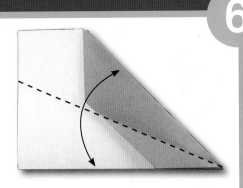

Valley fold the top wing to the bottom edge and unfold. Repeat this step on the back wing.

7

Valley fold the bottom-left corner up. Note how the corner meets the top flap's short edge. Make a firm fold and then unfold.

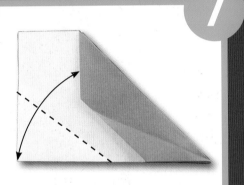

8

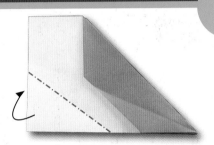

Inside reverse fold the bottom-left corner on the folds from step 7. This fold allows the bottom edge to swing inside the model.

9

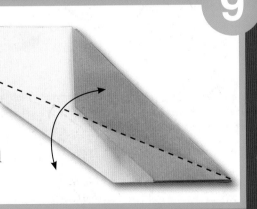

Valley fold both wings on the folds from step 6. Unfold the wings halfway.

10

You've earned your wings! Give your plane a test flight.

PLAY hint Pinch the bottom of the air shark with your fingers. Send it soaring with a smooth, level throw.

MINI piano

Traditional model

Impress your friends with this mini piano. Make it fancy by folding it in black paper. Or try red, green, or yellow paper for a fun, playful look.

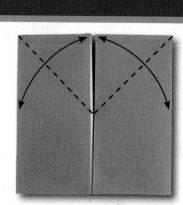

1 Start with the coloured side of the paper face down. Valley fold the left edge to the right edge and unfold.

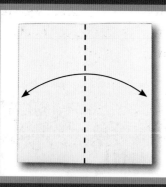

2 Valley fold the top edge to the bottom edge.

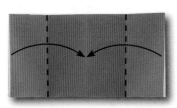

3 Valley fold the left and right edges to the centre fold. You now have two tall flaps on top of the model.

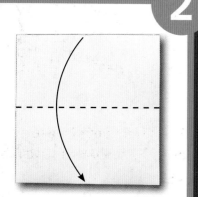

4 Take the left flap and valley fold its top inside corner to the left edge. Make a firm fold and then unfold. Repeat this step on the right flap.

5

Squash fold the left flap. Make this fold by flattening the top inside corner on the folds from step 4. Repeat this step on the right flap.

6

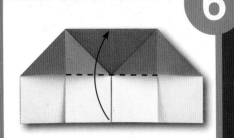

Take the top layer and valley fold its bottom edge to the model's top edge.

7

Take the top layer and valley fold its top edge to the middle edge. Make a firm fold and unfold.

8

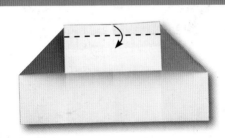

Valley fold the top layer again. This time the top edge meets the fold from step 7.

9

Valley fold the top layer one more time. This fold is made on the fold from step 7.

10

Valley fold the left and right edges to the centre fold. Unfold the edges halfway. Then lower the top layer to form the keyboard.

11

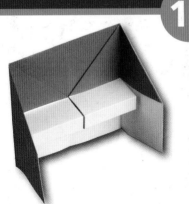

Your mini piano is ready for its keys. Draw the piano keys with a black pen.

 **PLAY hint** Pretend you are giving a concert in the park. Do you need seating for the audience? Make a second model, but don't colour in the keys. You can use this model as a park bench.

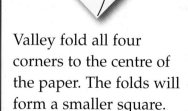

SUMO wrestler

Traditional model

You don't have to visit Japan to see the power of sumo wrestlers. Fold your own wrestlers, and let them battle it out in the ring!

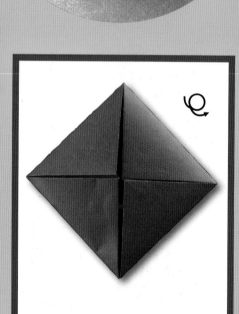

1

Start with the coloured side of the paper face down. Valley fold the left point to the right point and unfold. Valley fold the top point to the bottom point and unfold.

2

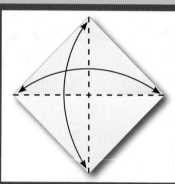

Valley fold all four corners to the centre of the paper. The folds will form a smaller square.

3

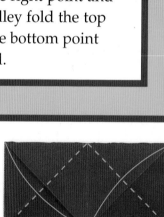

Valley fold all four corners of the smaller square to the centre of the paper.

4

Turn the model over.

5

Valley fold the top-left edge to the centre fold. Allow the flap behind the edge to swing to the front. Repeat this step on the top-right edge.

6

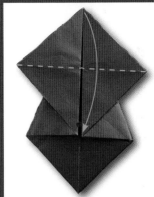

Valley fold the top point down to meet the middle point. Allow the flap behind the point to swing to the front.

7

Mountain fold the bottom point behind the model.

8

Valley fold the right side of the model to the left side.

9

Valley fold the triangle-shaped flap at the bottom of the model. Make this fold by opening the left side of the model and pulling the tip of the flap down. Then close the model and allow the flap to valley fold in half.

10

Your sumo wrestler is ready to rumble!

PLAY hint

Draw a large circle in the middle of a notebook. Place two sumo wrestlers in the centre of the circle. Slide one end of the notebook over the edge of the table. Tap the overhanging part of the notebook rapidly. The first wrestler to fall down or cross the edge of the circle loses the match.

BUG-EYED darting frog

Traditional model

The bug-eyed darting frog would rather run than hop. This model is built for speed and is ready to race!

1

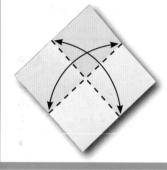

Start with the coloured side of the paper face down. Valley fold the bottom-left edge to the top-right edge and unfold. Valley fold the bottom-right edge to the top-left edge and unfold.

2

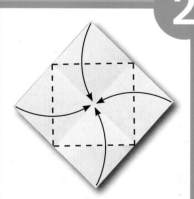

Valley fold all four points to the centre of the paper to form a smaller square.

3

Mountain fold the top corners behind the model. The corners should meet the centre of the model.

4

Valley fold the left and right edges to the centre of the model.

5

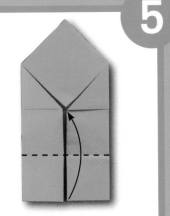

Valley fold the bottom edge to the centre edge.

6

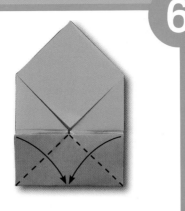

Valley fold the corners of the top layer to the bottom edge.

7

Pinch the tops of the triangles from step 6. Gently pull the top layers of these triangles out to the sides of the model. Two pointed feet will form.

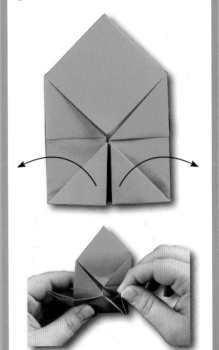

8

Turn the model over.

9

Valley fold the left inside corner to the left edge and unfold. Valley fold the right inside corner to the right edge and unfold.

10

Open the slit of the left inside corner. Squash fold on the folds from step 9 to form a rectangle-shaped eye. Repeat this step on the right inside corner.

11

The race is on! See how fast your bug-eyed darting frog can run.

PLAY hint
Place two frogs side by side on a table. At the same time, you and a friend must blow on the back ends of your frogs. The first frog to dart all the way across the table wins.

Origami PLAYTIME

READ more

My First Origami Book: Things That Go, Nick Robinson (Dover Publications, 2012)

Origami for Children, Mari Ono and Roshin Ono (Cico, 2008)

Origami Ooh La La!: Origami for Performance and Play, Jeremy Shafer (Createspace, 2010)

Origami Zoo: An Amazing Collection of Folded Paper Animals, Robert J. Lang (St. Martin's Griffin, 2006)

INTERNET sites

You can find other interesting origami models on the websites below, along with step-by-step guides on how to make each model.

www.activityvillage.co.uk/origami_for_kids.htm

www.enchantedlearning.com/crafts/origami/

ALPHA

DISCARDED

014151207 2